re · sil · ient

How to Bounce Back From Loss

Jason Scales

ISBN 9780692588154

Published In Part by:

KEEN VISION

Cover Illustration Copyright © 2015 by Jason Scales
Cover design by Cary Kelley
Editing by Keen Vision

Limits of Liability and Disclaimer of Warranty

The author and publisher shall not be liable for your misuse of this material. This book is strictly for informational and educational purposes. The purpose of this book is to educate and entertain. The author and/or publisher do not guarantee that anyone following these techniques, suggestions, tips, ideas, or strategies will become successful. The author and/or publisher shall have neither liability nor responsibility to anyone with respect to any loss or damage caused, or alleged to be caused, directly or indirectly by the information contained in this book.

In Loving Memory of my Siblings,

Jonathan Scales & Jessica Moss

Also, this book is dedicated to my wife and my son, parents, nieces and nephews, Big Mama (grandmother), aunts and uncles, all of my cousins, in-laws, and close friends. Thank you all for your support and I sincerely love you all!!

Much love to the greatest church and staff in the world, Believers Faith Fellowship!

MEET THE AUTHOR

Jason D. Scales is a native of Shelbyville, TN. He currently resides in Murfreesboro, TN. He earned a B.S. in Psychology and MBA at the University of Tennessee at Chattanooga. He is married to Barbara A. Scales and the proud father of Isaiah Scales. Pastor Scales founded the Believers Faith Fellowship Church in January 2009. Pastor Scales has a heart to teach people with simplicity and power. His desire is for everyone to have an intimate relationship with Jesus Christ, be passionate in their worship, sincere in their praise, wise in their decision making, and purposeful in their living.

CONTENTS

Introduction

re-sil-ient: *Able to become strong, healthy, or successful again after something bad happens; Able to return to an original shape after being pulled, stretched, pressed, bent, etc.*

I was raised in good 'ole Shelbyville, TN by my parents, Wayne and Shelia Scales. They are truly the most re•sil•ient people I've ever met. For a while, my mother was the only lady in the house. I had a brother named Jonathan, who was three years younger than I was. Eventually, mom got tired of the burping battles, farting contests, and constant wrestling - you know, the typical joys of having a house full of males. Around my seventh-grade year, my parents adopted my sister, Jessica. Jessica's entrance into our family changed our lives in ways we never imagined. I vividly remember the day my parents brought her home. We fell in love with her instantly. To this day, Jessica is still one of the prettiest and most talented ladies I have ever met. As an older brother, I didn't know how to share my emotions, but Jessica had undoubtedly stolen my heart. I loved that she was always so strong-willed and independent. I was amazed at her growth and maturity. In 2009, she and her family prepared to move to Montana. Jessica had gotten married, and her husband had enlisted in the Air Force. A couple of days before their departure, we lost Jessica in a tragic car accident. She was only twenty-years-old. She and her six-week-old son were just leaving the doctor's office. Miraculously, he survived the wreck. She left behind a husband, two children, a mother, father, two brothers, and a host of family, friends, and loved ones. After this tragedy had taken place, we were devastated. It took a drastic toll on her husband and my parents. I can still remember the pained looks on their faces. To this day, the reality of her death is still hard to grasp. As her pastor, I had

the challenge of delivering her eulogy. I had never given a
eulogy at a funeral. I'd never liked funerals, in fact, I am
still traumatized from having to carry the casket of a child
who had died of pneumonia when I was in the fifth grade.
Can you imagine me standing over my sister's coffin,
attempting to deliver my first eulogy? The burden was
tremendous. By the grace of God, my family and I made it
through that day. The night before the funeral, my brother,
Jonathan, and I had sat in a parking lot at a local park and
prayed. He encouraged me to preach the eulogy. Jonathan
always had a way of calling me at the right time and knowing
what to pray. Jonathan was my best friend and one of my
biggest supporters. We went from fighting as kids to being
the best of friends as adults. We had an incredible bond. He
and I talked at least three to four times a day. I remember
riding in my car one day after the funeral. I had just hung up
from talking to Jonathan, and a random thought hit me. I
remember saying to myself, "I don't know what I would do

if I lost my brother too." In September of 2010, I got a call from my mom telling me my sister-in-law had found my brother lying dead on the bathroom floor. My sister-in-law had awakened early in the morning and noticed that my brother was not in their bedroom. She had heard him get up to use the restroom earlier in the night but didn't remember him coming back to bed. Slightly alarmed, but not overly concerned, she went to look for him. That's when she saw Jonathan lying lifeless on the floor of their bathroom. That's right. Eleven months after the death of my sister, one of my greatest fears happened. I was broken. My world had been torn apart. I had just talked to Jonathan the night before, and he seemed perfectly fine. He left behind a wife and a baby, who was only a couple of months old. It never occurred to me that one day as an adult I would be the only remaining child of my parents. To this day, birthday parties, holidays, and other family events are hard. I constantly battle "survivor's remorse". It has been tough to experience life with my wife and son while watching Jonathan's and Jessica's families live life without them. Those experiences opened my eyes to the reality of loss, and the impact it has on people.

This book gives insight on my journey through recovering from loss. I pray it will help you become more resilient and teach you how to bounce back from obstacles that you have and will face in life. Life will often throw things that knock us down, but we have the choice to get up and push forward. Within this book, I will give you the tools needed to realize that God designed us to be RESILIENT. Discussing the subject of loss may seem anti-inspirational, anti-motivational, and even anti-faith. Understand that having faith doesn't mean everything goes as planned or without a hitch. Being a person of faith doesn't exempt you from loss or setbacks. I consider myself a strong man of faith. I have seen God do some things that are beyond my comprehension. However, I have experienced some pretty tough losses that made me question my faith. Through some tough experiences, I have learned the true meaning of faith and how it allows you to handle loss and emerge victoriously.

Perhaps you have experienced the loss of loved ones, jobs, physical ability, money, or failed relationships. Can I ask you a question? Has anyone ever taught you how to lose? Probably not. As Christians, we are taught how to gain things, how to get a job, find a spouse, buy a house, or even a car. But, we don't always win in every situation, now do we? The harsh reality of losing things is not one that we train ourselves to handle. We seek prosperity, but it is rare that we discuss how to endure in the face of adversity. My prayer is that you allow this book to serve notice that even though you may have lost a few battles, the war can still be won.

iWin

I have a tremendous sweet tooth. Luckily for me, I am blessed to be surrounded by some of the best cooks in the world. One of my friend's mother makes a lemon pound cake with a lemon glaze that is phenomenal. Whenever she makes it I eat several pieces at a time. I liked it so much that I talked her into giving me the recipe. I was overjoyed when she finally released the secret of that savory goodness.   The first time I made the cake it tasted nothing like when my friend's mother made the cake. I was sure she left out the family secret behind the recipe. To my surprise, she had not. It took several attempts, but I eventually got it right.

In the process of perfecting the cake, I realized that no matter how bad my attempts tasted, it did not ruin the recipe. The more I practiced and asked questions, the more my skills increased. My determination allowed me to produce a cake that reflected what the recipe had the potential to be. Life is pretty much the same. Being a winner in life reflects my process of learning how to bring the potential out the recipe to make that cake. We are perfectly made.   Our identities as winners are established because of who made us. There is nothing we can do to

> *We are **human beings**, not **human doings**. Our confidence is based upon who we are – not how we feel.*

ruin that. We can't ruin perfection. We practice perfection. Every day is a new day to practice perfection and get it right. Winning is learning how to practice perfection. A win is getting it right and a loss is getting perfection wrong. Neither adds or takes away from perfection. Making mistakes does not ruin our lives. We have problems, but we are not the problem. Jesus Christ has already overcome everything we will ever face. We are living in His victory. This is why we are winners. It can be disappointing to lose. Even the most resilient people experience disappointment, but here's the difference – their confidence is not impacted by whether they lose or win, pass or fail. They are confident in knowing that failure only provides another opportunity to get it right!

Let's discuss how to establish our identities as winners. First things first: What does it mean to win? We often feel like we must gain something to be a winner. This is not true. We must change our mindsets of viewing wins as tangible prosperity. Winning is more than visual success. Our performance doesn't make us winners. The awards, properties, and assets we have accumulated do not define us as winners and a lack of these things do not make us losers. Winning is the position in which we operate in our lives. Winning is our identity. Here's the thing. Your position as a winner was established before you were born. We were designed to win! Jeremiah 29:11 states *"For I know what I have planned for you,"* *says the Lord. "I have plans to prosper you, not to harm you. I have* *plans to give you a future filled with hope."* No matter what we deal with in life, we must remember that we were created to be winners. Let's face it. We won't always come in first place. We will lose loved ones and people we hold dear. We will be heartbroken by people we once trusted. We may lose jobs and other prized possessions. These situations, however, DO NOT change our identities as winners.

THERE IS A WIN IN EVERY LOSS

When we suffer a loss, winning is the last thing on our minds. We put so much effort into dealing with the pain, the shock, and the never ending questions of *"why"* that we don't focus on pushing through. In the midst of trying situations, it's very difficult to see the win in our loss. This may sound very oxymoronic, but *there is* *a win in every loss.* Winning is **NOT** an anesthetic for heartache. Winning is **NOT** getting revenge, recovering what you have lost, or ignoring the loss altogether. Winning is first recognizing, then accepting the loss. Winning is learning how or why we lost in the first place. Winning is choosing to forgive even when our emotions say otherwise. Winning is making the decision to get up, strap up your laces, and keep moving forward. Being a winner means understanding that you are an overcomer because of your faith in Christ.

MADE TO WIN

Experiencing loss exposes great things about our hearts. Sometimes, we never know how strong we are until we have no choice but to be strong. As Christians, we become so concerned with God's view of us. Experiencing a loss of any type can cause us to question our faith and our belief. When God designed us, he knew we would not be perfect. He does not expect us to be perfect. God's desire is for us to become strong in our faith in Him. We must realize that God is not concerned about our immediate outcome. His biggest concern is that we learn from the different obstacles that may come our way. Internal lessons make us winners when the outward appearance of life suggests otherwise.

Think back to when you were in school, college, or maybe taking a test for a job. Can you recall those late nights of cramming tons of information hoping to receive a satisfactory grade? Ask yourself this, how much did you retain? Can you remember any of the information you crammed for the test? Probably not. We often get so caught up with passing the test that we don't take the time to actually learn the material and how to apply it.

> *Internal lessons make us winners when the outward appearance of life suggests otherwise.*

It can be disappointing to fail a test or lose. Even the most resilient people experience disappointment, but here's the difference – their confidence is not impacted by whether they lose or win, pass or fail. They are confident in knowing that failure only provides another opportunity to get it right!

God hardwired us with the innate ability to bounce back from adverse situations. We are made in the image of God. God put his very nature on the inside of us. That nature allows us to be resilient in any situation.

Have you ever heard of a *Weeble*? Many refer to this toy as a *"Weeble Wobble"*. The slogan for the *Weeble* is, "It may weeble, it may wobble, but it won't fall down." *Weebles* are designed to always bounce back to an upright position – no matter how hard they are pushed. Believers of Jesus Christ are like the *Weeble*. We may weeble and wobble, but when our faith is strong in Jesus Christ, we won't stay down. Because of its design, gravitational pull always brings the *Weeble* back to its upright position. Our resilient nature can cause us to always bounce back to our posture as winners. Note the words **"can cause"** versus **"will cause"**. The *Weeble* has no choice but to bounce back. It doesn't have free will. Its design puts it at the mercy of gravitational pull. As human beings, however, *we have free will*. We decide if we will allow our resilient nature to come forth in our lives.

Do you have a smartphone? If so, check out the settings of your GPS. The GPS can direct you wherever you desire to go. It was built into your phone, but it only works if you enable the feature and follow the directions. The same is true with resilience. We were built with resilience, but it only works if we allow it to do so.

Another issue we as Christians face is believing that dealing with tough situations makes us unrighteous. The reality is you bounce from unrighteousness because you are righteous. That's another book. However, condemnation keeps so many Christians from rising above their current situations. Redemption is free, we only have to receive it. Again, God does not expect us to be flawless. Bouncing back is not tied to our performance. Bouncing back is tied to our identity. If bouncing back were tied to our performance, many of us wouldn't be here today. Take a look at your life. You haven't dotted every "i" and crossed every "t". You have dealt with some pretty rough things, but they did not kill you. Not because you were so deserving of a second chance, but because God's grace and mercy saw fit to grant you another opportunity. Just like the gravitational pull that allows the *Weeble* to bounce back, God's grace and mercy are ours for the taking. It flows abundantly if we choose to accept it and do better.

In my life, with the help of God's grace and mercy, I made the decision to bounce back from the loss of my siblings and everything that came after that. I decided to trust God and not my own ability. I learned to lean on God, and not my own strength. I realized that I had to rely on God's will instead of my own intelligence. Take a look at John 16:33 (NLT). In this scripture, Jesus was preparing to be crucified. He was upfront with his disciples. He told them they would have to face hard things in life, but He assured them that if they trusted in Him they would be ok. Jesus' exact words in scripture were, *"I have told you all this so that you may have peace in me. Here on earth, you will have many trials and sorrows. But take heart, because I have overcome the world."*

What does this scripture say to us as Christians of this day and age? The exact same thing. The scripture never said that life would be easy, but it does let us know that because Jesus overcame the world, *so can we.* We have to look to Him. He is our strength and our Redeemer. He won so that we could be winners.

It's natural to sometimes feel like a big-time loser, but we must remember that our feelings are not indicators of who we are. God's love is so consistent. It remains the same, even when our faith wavers. Our feelings may change due to loss, but a loss does not change our identities. Our obstacles do not have the power to change who we are.

*My situation **does not change the way He wired me**, but the way He wired me **has the power to transform my situation.***

Imagine a product being made by a manufacturer. Let's just say a television. Before the TV hits the market, it is checked to ensure it is ready to be used under any condition. The manufacturer checks for any problems that may have occurred during the manufacturing so that when the TV is bought, it will serve its purpose. Even though the manufacturer thoroughly checks the TV, they are not perfect. This why manufacturers provide warranties for their products. They make a commitment to the buyer that if the product doesn't work, they will repair it or replace it. The only thing manufacturers won't cover is the intentional abuse of their product. So if you drop that TV while attempting to move it, you just have a broken TV. Here is the great thing about God; He is perfect, but He knew we wouldn't be perfect! He provided us with a warranty, not in fear that He may have messed up, but because He knew that we would mess up! And get this – His warranty covers us even when the abuse is self-inflicted and intentional. Aren't you glad to know that you are covered no matter how many times you fall or get knocked down?

One of the greatest things I have learned about God is that He is *with me*. He wants to engage in every part of my life. However, He will only engage to the extent that I allow Him. He is just as much *with me* now as He will ever be. My condition doesn't reflect how *"with me"* He is. He is *with me* in low moments and in high moments. He is *with me* if I have money or down to my last dime. My situation does not change the way He wired me, but the way He wired me has the power to transform my situation. Knowing that

God is *with me* gives me the confidence to face any situation because I know HE is there.

Genesis 1:26 tells us that we were made in the image of God. We were pressed, fashioned, and squeezed to look like Him mentally, physically, and spiritually. God is not a loser, and neither are we. God built us to be resilient! He made sure we had the supernatural ability to bounce back. This is why it is so hard to quit or throw in the towel. There is something programmed inside of us that won't let us quit. Resilience is the drive that will not allow us to settle. This is why we become conflicted after settling for second best. It is not in our nature to struggle or barely make it. Somewhere deep down inside, we want to be the best at everything that we do. We fail to realize that the word best is NOT a *quantitative term* (meaning you win first, second, or third place). The word best is a *qualitative term* meaning REGARDLESS of the situation, *you* are striving to be the best *you* that God created *you* to be. Not in comparison to anyone else, but in comparison to all God says *you* can be.

THINK LIKE A WINNER

We have been ID'd as winners, designed as winners, and wired as winners. Finally, to establish ourselves as winners, *we have to think like winners.* There is a distinct difference between a *thought* and *thinking.* Have you ever been sitting and suddenly a friend, a family member, a bill, or a task pops into your head? Well, that's a *thought. Thinking* is when you allow a thought to stay and linger. Pretty simple, right?

Take a look at this example:

Thought: *"I just bought a house, what if I lose my job?"*

Thinking: *Did I turn in my reports? How did my boss respond to me yesterday? Did I do everything right? Is my coworker out for me? Am I really good at what I do? I'm sure someone else could do it better. What if they already have someone lined up? They're having a meeting...I wasn't invited. Was it about me? How stupid of me. I should not have made that purchase. Now, I'm going to lose my job.*

Outcome: *At work, I can no longer focus on doing my job. Now, I am so concerned with watching everyone, watching my boss, and preparing to be fired that I make simple mistakes. Thinking about losing keeps me up at night. So now, I've been written up for being late. My boss calls me in to discuss my performance at work. He thinks that I am no longer a good fit for my position. I've been demoted.*

The example above shows how a negative thought can impact our lives. Take a look at the second example:

Thought: *I am so happy at my job even though my current position doesn't pay much.*

Thinking: *I wonder what I can do to perform better. Sure, my coworkers erk my nerves every now and then, but they're pretty good people. I do wish I made more money, but I'll get there. I know I will. I just have to keep pushing. In the meantime, God will provide.*

Outcome: *I get to work on time every day. I wake up with anticipation to get to my job and do my very best. I work well* *with my teammates. Together, we get the job done. My boss notices my ingenuity and my creativity. I get promoted to higher paying position. My hard work pays off.*

Thoughts are always popping in and out of our minds. *Thoughts* can be positive of negative. However, the

> Don't allow every thought that **pops in** to **move in**.

thinking that goes into a thought is what produces action. Some thoughts will inspire you to push ahead while others may convince you to stop in your tracks. Don't allow every thought that pops in to move in. Be careful of the thoughts you allow to take residence in your mind. Negative thoughts have no place in the mind of a winner. The enemy wants us to believe that we won't make it, *that's a lie.* The enemy wants to convince us that can't we get over a loss, *that's a lie.* The enemy even wants us to think that God has forsaken us, *THAT IS A LIE.* However, if we allow negative thoughts such as these to take residence in our minds, we begin to believe every word the enemy says. Philippians 4:8 says, "Finally, brothers, whatever is true, whatever is honorable, whatever is just, whatever is pure, whatever is lovely, whatever is commendable, if there is any excellence, if there is anything worthy of praise, think about these things."

You choose what you will think on. Whatever you think on is what you will become. Whenever you get discouraged, bombard your mind with things that reinforce what you believe. Surround yourself with people of faith and listen to inspiring sermons and music. Rid your mind of idle thoughts and do some intentional thinking. This is what the Bible calls *renewing the mind*. The greatest battle of our faith occurs in our mind. Once we win the battle in our mind, the other battles aren't so difficult to survive.

iWin, youWin, weWin!

We are all winners in Christ. Once we accept our positions as winners, nothing in life can hold us back. As winners, we recognize that every delay in our desires, every let-down, every death, every loss, every failing grade, every past-due bill, every heartache, and every pain works for our ultimate gain. Child of God, you are a winner. You are the only one who can forfeit your position as a winner. Whenever you feel like you can't make it, just think about how far you've already come. Remember to think positively and evict every negative thought that moves into your mind. Push past your past, and accept your bright future. Your current circumstances don't define you. Your faith in Christ deems you a *winner*. Accept your position and win!

Loss vs Lost

The words 'loss' and 'lost' are very common and often misunderstood to be the same.

Loss: The fact or process of losing something or someone

Ex. Due to a house fire, the family suffered a great loss.

Lost: Used to describe items or situations that cannot be recovered; final; unable to find one's way

Ex. Even though they practiced hard, the team lost the championship this year.

As you can see, these words have two *totally* different meanings. Realizing their differences will help you view life's obstacles in a different light. Many times, we try to recover what we *lost*, which is often impossible. A *loss*, on the other hand, can be recovered and rebounded from. The purpose of this book is to focus on how to rebound from a loss, not focusing on what we lost.

> *Suffering a **loss** does not mean you have **lost**. Learn the **difference**.*

Losses fall into two categories:

Self-inflicted: Losses that happen as a result of our choices. This type of loss can be positive or negative.

Unavoidable: Losses that are out of our control.

SELF-INFLICTED LOSS	UNAVOIDABLE LOSS
Losing a job because of tardiness.(*Negative*)	Inability to use limbs due to age, sickness, or health.
Walking away from a job to pursue entrepreneurship. (*Positive*)	Being laid off a job due to company downsizing.
Failing a test due to lack of studying. (Negative)	Loss of loved ones due to death.

UNAVOIDABLE LOSS

Every now and then, life can throw a hard one. Sometimes we are

hit with losses that literally knock the wind out of us. When we get

laid off a job, when a spouse no longer wants the marriage, or when

we lose loved ones we often feel left alone to pick up the pieces.

Unavoidable losses leave us in tough situations. Sure, we have

ibuprofen for body pain, beta blockers for blood pressure, or insulin

for diabetes, but *what can we take to heal a broken heart*? A loss in

this capacity impacts our faith. It causes us to become uncertain. It hinders our ability to trust. After suffering unavoidable losses, we spend a lot of time blaming ourselves. We question where things went wrong. We constantly wonder what we *would have, could have,* or *should have done.* The hardest part about unavoidable losses is the helplessness we feel as a result of the situation.

SELF-INFLICTED LOSS

Some self-inflicted losses are positive while others are negative. Self-inflicted losses can be difficult to deal with. Hindsight is always 20/20. After we've made bad choices and reaped the consequences, we are able to see our mistakes clearly. We are able to look back and realize what we should have done. Seeing our mistakes and wishing we could have done things differently can be very disappointing.

Whether our losses are *unavoidable* or *self-inflicted,* God's grace is still sufficient. God doesn't care how we get in situations. *His only concern is that we get out of them.*

I love reading about Jesus' encounters with people throughout the Bible. I never once saw Him interrogate a person or belittle them because of their situation. Once He saw their faith, He moved to heal and deliver them.

Despite our situations, God is able to restore us and push us FORWARD. For any type of loss in our lives, Jesus Christ is able to help us regain our identities as winners. Again, he's not concerned with how we got there. He is concerned about freeing us from the bondage of a loss and launching us into winning.

> *God doesn't care **how** we get into situations. His only concern is that **we get out of them**.*

WHEN LOSING LEADS TO MORE LOSING

Sometimes it feels like as soon as we get over one thing, along comes something else. It feels like we can barely catch our breath before life throws another punch. Losing back to back is tough. Instances of repetitive losses can impact our confidence and psyche.

The enemy plays on our repetitive losses by making us feel like we are destined to lose.

After we lose, it is important to do an *autopsy* on the loss. We must take time to see *why* it happened, not *what* happened. As long as we have breath in our bodies, we will get another opportunity to win. In the meantime, we need to understand why we keep rehearsing loss.

I remember being a physical therapy major in college. I got a job as a physical therapy technician and had connected with a hospital that would pay my tuition to PT (physical therapy) school. I was pumped. I applied three times to physical therapy school, but I didn't get in. I got an interview each time and even made the alternate list. I was *crushed*. The last time I applied, I was a senior in undergraduate school. I was embarrassed and without direction. In my mind, I kept going through all the reasons I didn't get in. Maybe it was my race. Maybe it was the enemy. Maybe it wasn't my time. Finally, I got tired of pondering and decided to call the PT department. I talked with the head of the physical therapy department and asked him candidly why I didn't get in and what I needed to improve upon. He told me something I couldn't believe. He said I scored very low in my interview. I was in shock. I am a public speaker. I speak in front of people all the time. I assumed that I was an effective communicator. Through this instance, I discovered that public speaking and interviewing are two distinct entities. The head of the physical therapy department encouraged me to work on my interviewing skills and apply again. I made a decision not to apply again. I chose to move on. However, I learned an important lesson about understanding loss.

Here are a few questions to ask yourself after a loss:

Did I desire to win?

If you've suffered a self-inflicted lost, take a look at your system. Oftentimes, our systems (how we operate) don't reflect our desire to win. Do you desire to win? Are you living your life in a way that makes winning possible?

Did I prepare to win?

Maybe your system lacks the preparation to win. When we aren't prepared to win, we lose again and again. It's very frustrating when what we're experiencing in life differs from what we believe God for.

Did I believe I could win?

We frequently go into situations believing that we will lose. When we go into situations feeling defeated, we have already lost. We have to remember to face each situation with a fresh look.

Many of you reading this book have suffered repetitive losses. Maybe you've been passed over for a promotion you feel you deserved. Maybe you're never asked to serve on committees at work or church. Maybe everyone around you

> *When we aren't prepared to **win**, we **lose** again and again.*

seems to be finding companions and you're always the third wheel. I want to challenge you to ask your boss or those closest to you candid questions about yourself and take their answers to heart. Don't internalize their responses. Always remember that there is a difference between *having a problem* and *being the problem.* Use their responses as a tool to grow and *not* as a reflection of who you are as a person. Constructive criticism is only a correction of behavior, not a correction of identity. Remember your identity is set as a winner.

LOSING FOR A PURPOSE

Sometimes we must endure periods of suffering to accomplish a goal. Athletes must condition their bodies for the season. Your desired career may require a college education or an intense period of training that may take months or years. Starting a business requires financial and time-consuming sacrifices. The suffering endured during these trying moments is necessary to achieve the goal that has been set. When people decide to get out of debt, they sacrifice vacations, certain luxuries, buying new cars, shopping for clothes, etc. When people decide to lose weight, they give up their favorite foods, relaxation, and their comfort level. Some people and things we lose are a win because of the unhealthy connections we have with them. During these times of intentional loss, we press for the joy set before us. Jesus Christ endured the cross and despised the shame for the joy set before Him. He knew that what He went through would be worth it. He was going somewhere. We have to live our lives the same way. What is the joy set before you? What do you have to look forward to after this period of loss? When you have a joy set before you, it becomes your motivation to keep pushing. This motivation can be simple. It could be walking up a flight of

> *When you have a joy set before you, it becomes your **motivation** to keep pushing.*

steps without becoming winded. It could be turning on your home phone because you are not avoiding bill collectors. It could be a cruise or a great vacation. You may go ahead and buy the picture frame or pick a place on the wall for that degree. You may buy a dress in your desired size and put it in your closet so you see it every day. I challenge you to set a goal. Understand that loss may be a necessary part of your journey, but it will be worth it. You have joy set before you.

LOSING TO LEAD

I recall talking with one of my pastoral mentors and he made a statement I live by as a leader. He said, "Sometimes you have to lose to lead." He told me that he tells his staff, "You are just as important as anybody, but you are not more important than everybody." He meant we will do everything we can to care for you, develop you, and include you, but when you are sabotaging the culture of the entire group because you want to do your own thing, some decisions will have to be made.

Within any organization, everything rises and falls with *leadership*. Leadership is all about influence and making tough decisions. Making decisions that will impact others takes courage. Some decisions are made for the growth of the entire organization.

A few years back, Coach Harbaugh of the San Francisco 49ers made a mid-season change to replace quarterback Alex Smith for Colin Kaepernick. I am sure it was hurtful to Alex Smith and seemed like a risky move for Coach Harbaugh. However, the move paid off. It earned the team a trip to the Super Bowl. The coach risked his reputation and I am sure many questioned his direction. The coach was faced with weighing loyalty versus growth. This is an area that is challenging for any organization.

In addition to growth, leaders have to make moves to protect the culture of their organization. Leaders often have to remove those who are talented, gifted, and smart because they are hinder the growth and flow of the organization. Making those tough decisions is difficult, but it is *necessary*. Tolerating certain behaviors and attitudes can often hinder the culture and the vision set for an organization. Leaders may have to take a loss of certain personnel or programs to steer things in the right direction.

> *As a leader, are you* ***tolerating*** *mediocrity,* ***pacifying*** *immaturity, or* ***delaying*** *the inevitable just to keep the* ***peace****?*

If you were to take a current evaluation of your life, organization, family, or entity in which you have influence, are there any areas you need to lose to have a victorious future? Are you tolerating mediocrity, pacifying immaturity, and delaying the inevitable just to keep peace? There are some things you must deal with now before it deals with you later. For some people, confronting issues is natural. For others, dealing with this type of loss is challenging. Regardless of your approach or feelings, sometimes losing is necessary. Ask God for the wisdom and courage to deal with any areas of your life where you need to lose to win. He will lead you to a place of victory and walk you through every step of the process.

God is not malicious or evil. When He leads you to do things, you live out Romans 8:28, "All things work together for the good of them that love the Lord and are called according to His purpose." Notice the key words in this scripture. It says all things meaning there is nothing left out. Every part of our lives are included in His plan. Also, notice it says, works together for the good of them. It doesn't say for you. It says for them. In every situation, things work together for the good of every party involved. God takes everyone's lives into consideration when He is orchestrating his purpose and plan. The only criterion required of us is that we love God. Love allows you to trust. Make a decision to trust God, understand the loss, and let Him work things out in your life.

Sore Losers

3

G rowing up, we had this one kid in our neighborhood who always got mad whenever he lost. I mean, the moment things didn't go his way, he would take his ball and go home. Everyone knew that if he lost, the game would be over. We would have avoided playing with him if it weren't for the fact that his ball was better than anyone else's. I'm sure many of you have encountered a similar kid at some point in your childhood. Taking the ball away after a loss was a form of control used to dominate situations. Sadly enough, this mentality doesn't end in with adolescence. Many adults still suffer from this syndrome. As soon as things don't go our way we "take our ball and go home". The result? High divorce rates, abandonment, rejection, and a bunch of broken promises. Most of us hate to lose. Since we don't know how to rebound from loss, we continue to lose.

Loss is not a popular topic in many Christian circles. Many of us don't want to lose anything but a few pounds and people that get on our nerves. We are people of faith. We don't lose anything. We are all about gain. Losing is taboo and shouldn't be a part of our lives, right? Wrong! The truth of the matter is, we lose every day, and many of us are sore losers.

I have a young son who pouts each time he loses. I get on to him all the time about it. He gets upset when he loses a Wii game and insists that the game is cheating. I realized the source of his anger. He is a winner. He has the drive to be on top. I never want him to lose that drive. However, it is my responsibility to teach him how to bounce back from a loss and use that drive to win. I never want him to get used to losing, but I want him to realize that even in losing, things will always work out for his good.

*How we respond to loss **impacts** our next win.*

Don't get me wrong, I did the same thing when I was a kid. I can't tell you how many fights my brother and I got into because we both hated to lose. When we played Nintendo, whoever was losing would get mad, hit the reset button, and start the game over. To this day, I hate to lose, but the reality is we are losing every day. We lose a step athletically; we lose hair, and we lose our memory, just to name a few things. Here is a hard reality to face: You don't win every time you play, but that doesn't take away from who you are. One loss doesn't make you a loser. We have to learn how to get wisdom from our losses by rebounding from mistakes, becoming mentally tough, and developing the ability to congratulate our opponents when they outperform us. Am I advocating losing? Of course not. Things don't always go as planned, life happens. We must learn to reposition ourselves to be victorious.

I know a very wealthy man that lost a large sum of money. The type of money most will never see. He was upset, but he didn't shut down. The reason is, he knew how to make money. He knew if he made it once, he could make that and more again. Winners don't see a loss as permanent; we see it as temporary. We know life goes on, this is not the end, and things always work out.

LEARNING HOW TO TAKE AN "L"

Sore losers don't know how to take an "L". (In case you were wondering, an "L" is a loss). Think about this, most of us are taught how to gain things, but not how to lose things. Naturally, we are taught how to get a job, join a church, get married, buy a car, purchase a house, etc. Even though we don't always prepare to win, we never intentionally prepare to lose. As a result, when we are faced with loss we have the potential to end things very badly (in relationships, at churches, or on our jobs). Our society tells everyone "You can do anything you set your mind to". This is not reality. It is not even faith. You can't do anything you want to, but you can do what God has called you to do. I would love to sing and travel the world doing so. However, no matter how I set my mind to it, that will never be a reality. The truth is, everyone won't get the job, people get downsized, and everyone won't get promoted when they believe they should. Just because you don't get it now doesn't mean you won't ever get it. How you respond to your losses impact when ·you see your next win.

HANDLING CONFLICT AND CONFRONTATION

Sore losers struggle with handling conflict. People who handle conflict well move on easier from a loss. Those who fear conflict and confrontation take longer to recover from loss; that's if they ever recover. People who don't know how to handle conflict in a healthy manner confront everything emotionally instead of dealing with their emotions as they confront things. Our emotions tend to distort our view of situations and circumstances. If we allow our emotions to guide us, we are in for a LONG, ROCKY road.

So often, we run from conflict and deflect our feelings in other areas of our lives. We overwork, bring up issues that have nothing to do with the loss, or go into denial. During periods of loss, I have witnessed families fall part, marriages suffer, and friendships get volatile all because someone failed to confront the actual conflicts that arose as a result of the loss. I have seen brothers and sisters argue

> *When we make excuses, we relinquish our ability to change.*

when a parent dies because one felt they had always been treated differently. I've seen families argue over taking care of aging parents in assisted living or nursing home facilities. In these sensitive family disputes, both parties love each other and feel the same about the issue at hand, however, they lack the ability to confront the real issue. There is also a self-proclaimed martyr syndrome that can kick in. The self-proclaimed martyr syndrome is seen in a person who stays busy, takes on work for attention, and needs to be needed. They refuse to let people help because they subconsciously like the attention stress brings. This syndrome is actually a distraction during loss because it takes the focus off the loss and puts it on one individual. The attention is more on the stress than it is the stressor. This is why some people suffer from loss long after it has taken place. They deal with it for a prolonged period of time because, get ready, THEY NEVER DEAL WITH IT. As a result of not dealing with the real loss, they end up believing lies about people, themselves, or whatever the loss directly relates to. Everything for the rest of their life is seen through "loss-colored lenses".

For instance, let's say you experience loss in a relationship. If you don't deal with the person and issue at hand, you end up making other relationships pay for unresolved issues in the one you lost. It becomes easier to quit when things get tough, pout when you lose, justify fear and insecurity, and end up living a shell of the life you are supposed to live. Learn how to deal with conflict. Learn how to wisely confront situations and effectively deal with loss.

DROP THE LOSER MENTALITY

In a nutshell, your mentality is the way you think through situations. Sore losers have a loser mentality. During my high school basketball career, we were never able to defeat the Columbia Lions. During my senior year, they beat us four times. Here is the reality. We never won because we lost in our minds before we even walked out the locker room. This is how losing happens for Christians. We look at the opposition, and because we don't have a proper view of ourselves and our God, we count ourselves out before the game ever begins. There are many well-meaning people with a loser mentality. Just as losers, lose before they begin, Winners win before the game starts.

Once, I had a conversation with my brother about a certain situation I felt wasn't right. His response was simple. People know who they can mess with. He was right! When you are a winner, you don't put up with certain things. That doesn't mean you fight. This doesn't mean you are combative. It means you bring resolve to things and move on. The mentality of a loser always attracts drama. Drama never has an ending. It is a continuous saga on an emotional roller coaster. The loser mentality causes you to develop an addiction to drama with no idea that the common denominator in your dramatic situations is you. Losers always end up in the same spot. If we are not careful losing will turn into something it was never supposed to be, an identity.

A winner realizes that constantly blaming others allows the actions of others to dictate our response to life.

Those with the loser mentality are always looking for someone to blame for their situation. There is always an excuse. It is always someone else's fault. Here's the thing, when we make excuses, we lose the ability to impact change. Many people are legitimately victims of situations. People get hurt, taken advantage of, stolen from, etc. I have seen some resilient people go through extremely unfortunate things in life, yet choose not to be bitter. They let God heal them and proceed in life victoriously. People with the loser mentality face unfortunate things and paint themselves as the victim. It is their parents' fault, their church's fault, their ex's fault, their spouses' fault, or their boss' fault. Don't get me wrong, there are actual injustices in life, even winners are faced with them from time to time. A winner realizes that constantly blaming others allows the actions of others to dictate our response to life. When we constantly complain about what has been done to us, we give victimizers the steering wheel in our lives while we sit on stand-by in the passenger's seat. The victim mentality has an excuse for every bit of inactivity in life.

No matter what you are faced with, help is available. People with a victim mentality often lose because they do not ask for help. They take a passive role in life instead of being assertive to secure the help they need. People with a victim mentality realize that asking for help requires a level of responsibility and initiative. Asking for help after a tough loss is difficult because we are battling to regain control in our lives. Asking for help relinquishes control. We have to open up and hear the truth about ourselves. This may be difficult because we are subconsciously unsure if people are safe. We don't want to be hurt again, so we think the easiest thing to do is handle the loss alone and in our way. With a victim's mentality we assume that people don't understand, people don't care, and people will only judge. A victim's mentality makes life worse than it has to be.

*People **cannot** read your mind. They only know what's really going on in your life **if you tell them**.*

The victim mentality makes the people around us seem heartless and unconcerned. This mentality makes us assume that people can read our minds or intuitively know what is going on in our lives. As a result, we get defensive, pull away from healthy relationships, and gravitate toward people with the same problem as if they can help us. Please note, the victim mentality is much like the loser mentality. In fact, they are one in the same. Both always lose. Neither are positioned to win.

LOSERS vs WINNERS

Our thinking habits make the difference between whether we lose or win. Here are a few differences between the thinking of a loser and a winner.

The Loser	The Winner
• Looks for what's wrong and why things won't work before they even begin.	• Seeks for ways to make things work.
• Nit-picks and finds reasons to quit.	• Focuses and finds ways to win
• Only wins when everyone is off their back...when they have "peace".	• Can win under pressure
	• Faces conflict head-on
• Tip-toes around conflict	• Solution oriented
• Problem oriented	• Can work with anyone
• Has a hard time working with a team	• Works hard and doesn't care who gets credit

Be honest with yourself right now. How is your mind wired? Are you wired to see solutions or are problems always magnified in your eyes? Winners don't ignore the fact that problems exist. Winners see everything losers see, but they look beyond the problem to find the solution. Winners look to see if the situation can work. If they see a workable solution, they don't care who they must work with. They know if they work the solution, people issues will not be on the forefront. Winners want to win. Winners are not concerned about who gets the credit. They are secure in their identity. Their environments, the situations they are faced with, and the people around them don't interfere with who they are, nor do they determine how they act.

How do you know if you are currently suffering from a loser mentality? Complete this short self-checkup.

Do you see the worst in every situation?
Are you the victim in every situation?
Do people seem to offend you all the time?
Do you feel hurt, misunderstood, or taken advantage of?

Is everyone picking on you?

Do you find yourself fussing a lot?

Do you feel your boss or leader always attacking you?

If you answered yes to any of these questions, seriously consider if you are suffering from a loser mentality.

HOW TO BREAK THE LOSER MENTALITY

Below are a few ways that you can begin to break the loser mentality.

- Surround yourself with people who can help.

- Have an encounter with truth.

- Open your heart and mind to correction.

- Understand that one loss doesn't define you.

- Stop hosting your own pity party.

- Think like a winner.

The Impact

4

My phone rang. I answered it. It was my mother calling to tell me that my brother was dead. I remember that day as if it were yesterday. I was unexplainably broken. I remember being in a tearless, emotionless shock. I walked around my neighborhood and had what may seem like the most selfish conversation ever with God. I looked to heaven and said "God, I don't want to be next."

My ears couldn't believe what I had spoken aloud. I was gripped with fear and hurt. I am a Christian. I am a child of God. I know to be absent from the body is to be present with God, but I wasn't ready to go and I didn't want siblings to be gone either. It wasn't until that moment that I understood the concept of grief. I was sad when my sister passed, but when I lost both of them I felt like a part of me was missing. To this day, I still deal with the impact of those losses. I still find myself wanting to call them when something funny happens. I frequently fight the desire to call my brother when there is something on my mind. The deaths of my siblings opened my eyes to how loss impacts people in general.

Personally, I hate to lose at anything. I always want to win. I'm sure many of you are the same. Our desire to win makes grieving hard. We see a loss as the end of the world. I have met people who have had to downsize financially, transition in careers, or deal with the loss of physical strength and appearance. Losing what we've grown accustomed to takes significant adjustments. We miss the attention of the position, the freedom of financial stability, or the feeling of being physical fit. Oftentimes, we privately mourn over those things. Many of us even begin to secretly resent those who have what we once had.

The greatest impact of loss is the mismanagement of grief. Grief is a natural reaction to loss. Grief is caused by a change in a familiar pattern of behavior. Grief is real, and can even lead to depression. I never understood depression until I found myself going through it. One day, my wife gave me a call while she was driving. She said the car had begun to slow down. No matter how hard she pressed the accelerator, the car would not accelerate past a certain speed. She said that "Safe Mode" was displayed on the dash. We got the car towed to a mechanic.

Fear connects dots that have no business being connected.

The mechanic said, "Safe Mode" was the car's way of shutting itself down because something was wrong with its internal workings. If the car were allowed to go at higher rates of speed, it would have caused further damage.

In general, "Safe Mode" was the car's way of saying, "Fix me". God programmed our bodies the same way. When we go into depression, that is our bodies way of saying, "Fix me, address me, something is not working right." Depression carries such a bad stigma. Many Christians feel as though only evil, crazy, or "off" people deal with depression. For this reason, when we deal with depression, we don't seek help for it. Isn't it funny how we will go to the doctor and take medicine for anything physical, but become closed minded when it comes to seeking counsel for our mental health. Seriously, we can be on ten different medications for blood pressure, water retention, diabetes, and cholesterol, but at the mere mention of addressing our mental state with counseling and medication we are immediately turned off. If the doctor is good enough for your physical body, what's wrong with your mind?

It is impossible to deny the toll that grief takes on us. Many end up with drug addictions, alcohol dependency, emotional challenges, trust issues, bouts with depression, loss of sex drive, isolation, etc.

When we refuse to properly deal with grief and depression, the result can be catastrophic. We often begin to lose ourselves altogether.

A while back, I was selected to be the main speaker at a retreat. I remember encountering a young lady who dressed odd and acted very weirdly. The counselors at the retreat thought she had been possessed by a demon. One night after service, I heard a knock on my door. The counselors were frantically requesting me to pray for the young lady. Apparently, she was having one of her weird episodes.   Coming from a Pentecostal background, my initial response was to lay hands and cast the devil out of her. When I got ready to do this, the Lord spoke to me and led me through a series of questions to ask the young lady.   To my surprise, she was not demon possessed at all. She was grieving. She was angry with her mother who died and left her to live with her mother's boyfriend. The young lady felt rejected. She felt that she had no place in this world. It was tough being motherless because everyone around her had their mother. She was so often reminded that she was alone. The young lady's odd outward appearance was only her way of pulling away from the mainstream of society.

Grief is often misunderstood by both the griever and those around them. Greif can also bring about conflicted feelings. For instance, a person with a long-term illness dies and their caregiver is finally able to live and focus on life again. The caregiver is relieved that the deceased is no longer suffering. However, the caregiver is torn because they feel guilty about the joy of resuming their life.

In many instances when a person dies, there are unresolved issues with others that still linger. Those left to grieve are left with mixed emotions. How can you be mad at someone who is dead? Can you still resent the deceased if they broke your heart, lied to you, rejected you, or abandoned you? What do you do with those

> The death of a love one **does not** negate the fact that they hurt you!

feelings of anguish and pain left from a deceased loved one? Acknowledge them. Be honest about your emotions, but don't allow them to govern your actions. The impact of loss brings about many challenges. To effectively deal with loss, grief, and depression, we must learn how to handle a series of challenges.

CHALLENGE 1: IGNORANT ADVICE

During the death of my siblings, I overheard someone trying to encourage my parents by comparing them to Job. My issue was, Job lost ALL of his children, and my parents still had me. Perhaps I was a little sensitive and scared. Well, I was VERY sensitive and scared to be honest. However, for me and my faith, that wasn't what I needed to hear.

Some people feel the need to be "deep" during times of loss. Sometimes these deep people are blinded by their own issues, but still attempt to operate in the name of God. They abuse scriptures, overstep their boundaries, and convolute the grieving process.

Fear caused by grief can cause other dormant issues to surface.

During bereavement, people tend to offer their assistance more than they should because of the relationship they have with those who are experiencing loss. They feel as though they have to be the ones to pull them out of grief. Majority of the time, they are unqualified to do so and end up making the situation worse in the long run. If you are grieving or dealing with grief, think about this. Would you let a person who has not been to medical school perform surgery on your body? Probably not. You must take this same precaution when receiving advice on how to deal with loss. As a friend or loved one, know your limits. You may mean well, but many of us don't understand the process of grief well enough to give advice. Sometimes the best thing to say is nothing. Your presence may be the only thing they need.

CHALLENGE 2: FEAR

As a result of loss, many experience debilitating fears. As for me, losing my siblings made me afraid to have another child. Both of my siblings had children under 3 months of age when they died. I remember my wife and I discussing more kids and I had to be honest with her. The thought of leaving my children behind just as my siblings had terrified me. The two events had no correlation, but fear connects dots that have no business being connected. As a result of fear, many people exhibit isolation, numbness, loss of faith, being overprotective, paranoia, or uncontrollable anger (toward the person causing loss, toward God, or toward the person no longer here). Fear caused by grief can also cause other dormant issues that have nothing to do with the loss to surface.

CHALLENGE 3: FALSE TEACHINGS

Have you ever heard people say things like, "move on", "get over it", or "don't cry", "find something to replace your loss" or "keep busy"? These are the worst ways to deal with the impact of loss. The reality is you can't just move on or just get

> There's a difference between staying busy and working. **Work** produces results; **busy** just occupies time.

over it. Moving on is acting like something never happened! We can, however, move forward. Moving forward means life can proceed.   Even though we suffered loss, in moving on, we give ourselves permission to move ahead with life.

Crying is a natural emotion. Crying is not an indication that one is shutting down, stopping, and unstable. Our emotions are real and should not be ignored. They are an indication of our current state. Our emotions should not rule us, but they can be used as an indication of what is going on inside of us.

My wife and I lost our first child when Barbara was six months pregnant. Not long after that experience, we bought a dog. I love our dog to this day, but it can never replace what we lost. Many times, we do things to replace the loss instead of dealing with the loss. Sometimes people try to do it alone. Trust me, I get not wanting to be bothered during a time of any loss. I understand the need for personal quiet time. However, there is a significant difference between time alone and trying to handle things alone.   When Barbara and I left the hospital after losing our first child, my parents told us to meet them at Cracker Barrel. I really didn't have an appetite, but they insisted that I needed to eat. After a while at the restaurant, we were laughing and having a good time. I felt so guilty. I felt like we were supposed to be sad. We had planned to bring a kid home, but there we were childless in Cracker Barrel. To be honest, I needed that laugh. Being around people I loved and receiving love was healing for us. Going home and barricading ourselves with questions we had no answers to would have been a recipe for disaster. Many people try to be strong for everyone else and never give themselves a chance to grieve and receive restoration.

There's a difference between staying busy and working. Work produces results; busy just occupies time. People usually busy themselves as a way to offset the impact of loss. After the loss of my siblings, I continued to work in my calling. I found healing in my purpose, but I did not negate the fact that I needed to heal. No matter what type of loss you deal with, you must take the proper measures to deal with the impact in an effective way.

CHALLENGE 4: ENSHRINEMENT

After loss, our retrospective view of things may be off. Our sense of reality can easily become tainted. It is easy to get into enshrinement. Enshrinement is when we begin to obsess over memories and make sacred the valuables left behind by the deceased.

I knew a guy who had a piece of equipment that I wanted to use. He was very hesitant in letting me use it because it was one of the only memories he had left from a loved one. We talked and I assured him his loved one would want him to use it, as that is why they bought it in the first place.

Many times we think we should only think good thoughts about the deceased or things we have lost. As a result, we don't deal with the unresolved issues at hand. We tend to make people untouchable when they are gone. We act like everything they said and did was perfect. Here's the reality, they were not perfect, and neither are you. Their death doesn't negate the fact that they hurt you or issues may have been present. Being hurt or upset at someone who is deceased doesn't make you an evil person. It makes you human. It shows that you have feelings aside from their death that need to be resolved. You can be carrying things from a marriage that didn't work, a job you lost, or an athletic career that didn't pan out. That is okay. Deal with the things internally by taking responsibility for your feelings, instead of placing blame, and making the decision to move forward.

CHALLENGE 5: BEDEVILMENT

While some people enshrine people and things they lost, others move into bedevilment. They are unwilling to forgive and let go of disappointments and anger. They cling to the negative aspects of the relationship and they try to recover the wrong things. The reason many get caught in bedevilment is because they want revenge. They really don't want to heal, they want vengeance. This is often challenging and conflicting because many times the people these feelings are directed towards are dead, not in our lives, or in many instances have moved on, or are flourishing in their own lives.

Those are a few challenges that I have seen and perhaps you should consider them as you rebound from loss.

DEALING WITH THE IMPACT OF LOSS

Losing things has a tremendous impact on us. We must take a proper evaluation of ourselves and be honest about the impact of the things we've lost. In the event of an accident with your vehicle, the body shop normally does an assessment to estimate the damage done to the vehicle. The insurance assessor is not so concerned about who was at fault as he is figuring out the extent of the damage to determine what needs to be fixed and the cost of the repairs. We must do the same thing in the event of any type of loss, each person must assess the impact of the loss.

DEALING WITH THE IMPACT YOU CAUSED IN OTHERS

It is very easy to spend your days in guilt, condemnation, and misery because of loss, especially those that occur from the bad decisions we have made. When we repent, God forgives us in an instant. However, as humans, we must reconcile with others. Reconciliation is not a natural event. It is a divine movement of God. It requires the hand of God to heal and restore things. If you have caused damage, trust God's timing. Don't force the issue and expect others to automatically accept the changes you've made in your life. Your part is to make sure that your past is not a part of your current reality. Allow the same love of God that changed you to change the heart of others. It takes time to heal and reconcile because trust has been destroyed. Trust is behavioral, not verbal. It is something that is lived out, not talked out. You can ask a person to trust you all day, but until your actions line up with your words, you will never really see someone trust you. Trust is like a gift that can be retracted. Many people struggle with how to trust others or themselves. The only way to know if you can trust others or yourself is by taking a view of their relationship with Christ. Have they accepted Jesus Christ? Have they surrendered to being led by the Holy Spirit? A more tangible way to discern trust is viewing actions. A person who takes responsibility for their actions, doesn't make excuses for what they have done, or even try to justify their wrong is someone who is trustworthy. Trustworthy people aren't defensive about their past. They can admit when they have done wrong. They readily accept responsibility for their actions, aspire to become a credible person, and work hard to build the kind of life and relationships that are pleasing to God and are healthy for those around

> Allow the **same love of God** that changed you **to change the heart of others**. Move past the place of the **hurt** into a **place of healing**.

them. This is important because many people who have done wrong never regain the courage to stand in their rightful place as husbands, fathers, mothers, siblings, friends, pastors, leaders, etc. Doing wrong doesn't disqualify you from doing the right thing. With the help of God, you can regain your place in life. You can do it without a chip on your shoulder, guilt, regret, or even shame. If Jesus Christ has set you free, then you are free indeed. You can't go back and relive a day in your past. However, you can be freed from your past to experience the joy of your present. Every day is a gift from God. You can't enjoy today if you are still trying to recover yesterday. Every party involved in a loss has to make a decision to move forward to the present. Whatever happened, happened. You can't change it, as much as you may want to. Yes, it caused pain. No one is asking you to proceed like it didn't happen. Move past the place of the hurt into a place of healing. The enemy is an accuser. His job is to bring up accusations of things that have happened in life. What makes his lies so believable is that they hide behind facts. Yes, you have made mistakes. Yes, you probably did what he is accusing you of. Yes, you deserve the punishment that he is threatening you with. However, the enemy is a liar. You can know the truth and the truth will set you free. The truth is if any man be in Christ, he is a new creature. Old things are passed away and all things are new. There is nothing excluded from all. If you have received Jesus Christ in your life, you are a new creature and you have a fresh start. You can deal with the impact of loss and be resilient in everything you face. You are not that person anymore. That person that was hurt or caused pain does not exist anymore. You don't owe your past a thing. Your debt has been paid. Yes, you may have some difficult days ahead, but you will be resilient and get through them with the help of God.

Closure

F or something new to begin, something must end! Do you remember "boom boxes"? If not, a boom box was a music player that had a radio and cassette tape player. Some of them even had detachable speakers. Many people would walk around with them on their shoulders. The feature I loved most was the double-sided tape deck. You could take a tape and hit play

on one side and put a blank tape on the other side and hit "play &
record". They even got fancy and added a feature that would flip
sides for you, so you didn't have to stop the recording at the end of
the tape.   Back in the day, everyone had a mix tape with their
favorite songs on it.   One day, I ran out of tapes and had to use an
old tape that already had music on it. Let's

just say that didn't go too well. When I

finished "dubbing" the music I wanted on

my old tape I could hear two songs playing

at the same time. The sound was horrible.

> In order for something new to **begin**, something must **end**.

I couldn't hear the old song or the new song. Our lives are the same
way. We attempt to start something new on top of something old,
and because we can't make up our minds, we end up not being able
to enjoy neither.

UNTIL THE LAST BREATH

At a conference, I heard a scripture that changed my life. I was
very familiar with Abraham and his wife, Sarah, but I had never
considered Abraham's family. In Genesis 12, God tells Abraham to

leave his family and go to a place that He would show him. I took that scripture at face value until something from Genesis 11 jumped off the page to me. The Bible says this about Abraham's family:

(Genesis 11:27-28, 31) *"This is the account of Terah's family line. Terah became the father of Abram, Nahor and Haran. And Haran became the father of Lot. 28 While his father Terah was still alive, Haran died in Ur of the Chaldeans, in the land of his birth. 31 And Terah took Abram his son, and Lot the son of Haran his son's son, and Sarai his daughter in law, his son Abram's wife; and they went forth with them from Ur of the Chaldees, to go into the land of Canaan; and they came unto Haran, and dwelt there. 32 And the days of Terah were two hundred and five years: and Terah died in Haran."*

Abraham's (Abram) father's name was *Terah*. *Terah* had three sons. One son, in particular, was named *Haran*. *Haran* had died before his father died. No parent ever plans on burying their children. It is hard to comprehend. I know what it feels like to have lost two siblings, but I can't imagine what my parents felt. Genesis 11 concludes with the death of Abraham's father, and Genesis 12 picks up with God making a promise to Abraham and telling him to leave his kinsman. At the end of Genesis 11, *Terah*, Abraham's father, died in a place called *Haran*, the name of his deceased son. How ironic is it that the name of *Terah's* death place was the same as the name of his dead son, *Haran*?

Many of us stop living after we experience loss. We never see the promises of God because we *die* before we actually *stop breathing*. This loss could be a job that didn't go as planned, getting pregnant out of wedlock, loss of health, or divorce. Regardless of the type of loss, don't die in the place of your affliction.

So many of us have areas of our lives that stopped growing after we lost jobs, got divorced, lost loved ones, got rejected, or experienced trauma. We think we have advanced but because we didn't provide adequate closure, a part of us stopped living. It becomes obvious in how we raise our kids, deal with criticism, and respond to conflict and rejection. Instead of responding to current situations, we respond to the trauma in our life in which we didn't get closure.

FORGIVENESS

My wife and I went to a church conference and sat with another pastor and his wife. The pastor we sat with began to vent to me about a minister that had split his church and took half of his members. The pastor was obviously hurt by the situation. I could hear the anguish in his voice as he began to caution me about fickle people. He went on to advise me to guard myself. The pastor warned me that if I were not careful, the same thing would happen to me. His wife (who was his second wife whom he married after his first wife passed) looked at me and whispered, "The event my husband is talking about happened over ten years ago." At that moment, the Lord revealed to me that the pastor was not at the conference to grow his church. He was there to get his old church and members back. It was time for him to move forward. It was evident that he had enough in him to push through. After all, he had remarried after his first wife's death. He was resilient after that loss. The same principles that he used to move forward after the death of his first wife could be used to move forward from the split of his church. He needed to figure out where he was going, cast vision, and trust God to send people to carry out the vision. He didn't need to recover the church and members he once had, he needed to recover his confidence; his confidence in God, himself, and others.

Many times, we stop living because we are in *pursuit* of things we can't recover. Some questions may never be answered. You may never get an apology. You may never understand. And, that's okay. You don't need those things to move forward. You only need to grieve, forgive, and push forward. Forgiveness doesn't always require a conversation; it is a personal decision. Your decision to forgive *cannot* be predicated upon the actions of others.

I recall a young man who suffered because of the absence of his father. Even in his adult life, it hurt that his father never took him to the park, watched his ball games, or taught him life lessons. The void he felt in his heart made it difficult for him to move on. In cases such as these, God normally sends father figures to stand in the gap. He never leaves his children without. In order for the young man to receive the father figures God had blessed him with, he had to open his heart to receive that fatherly love, even though it didn't come from the source in which it should have. After his father had made the decision to come back into his life, he felt that he needed to make his father pay for the time lost. The young man had to realize that his father could never repay him for the time he was absent. Recanting and constantly talking about the childhood he never had wouldn't solve anything. The young man was only able to move forward after releasing the relationship from its prison of the past and allowing it to grow from the present.

UNRESOLVED FEELINGS, UNANSWERED QUESTIONS

What complicates closure more than anything is unresolved feelings and unanswered questions. Because of how my sister died, I never got to see her body after she died. Studies show that viewing a person's body after their death is a way of saying goodbye and a vital part of the grieving process. It makes it easier to accept the reality of death. The last memory I have of my sister is her showing up at church with her husband, son, and daughter. I never got closure in that sense, so I had to make a decision to cherish her memories.

Bringing closure to situations is a decision. I had to make several decisions along the way of my grief journey through loss. I had the choice to continue talking about death and the things I lost, or cherish the memories of my brother and sister. I decided to stop talking about their death and start talking about their life. I decided to live a

> God has something great in store **for you**, but you can't experience it in its fullness trying to play it over **old** stuff.

life that would make them proud. If it were me that passed, I would want them to live every day like it was their last. I would want them to grow in their relationship with God through Jesus Christ. I would not want them to be stunted by loss. I wouldn't want them to get tattoos with my name on it or create a shrine out of my pictures and memorabilia. I would want them to pursue their hearts' desires with everything in them. I would want them to employ the biblical principle of faith that I lived by. I would want them to laugh at the silly things we used to do. I would want them to tell stories of how we made the most of the time we had together. I wouldn't want them to waste their time on earth consumed with overcoming their loss of me. I would want them to live.

One day, about six months after my brother passed, I got ready to call him, and I was hit with sadness and despair over the fact that he wasn't there to answer the phone. At that moment, I cried out to God and asked him, "why?" Peace came over me, and it was like I heard something speak to my heart, "He's ok! If he had the chance to come back, he wouldn't. He is in paradise. He has no stress, sickness, worry, concerns. He is with the Father (God)!" I was overwhelmed and began to smile. I looked at myself in the mirror and said, "It's okay, man! Live!!" I felt all my heaviness lift. I didn't talk about his death or my sister's death much after that; I talked about their life. The dreams stopped and my perspective changed. I began to live again. I went home and apologized to my wife for all the times I was physically present, yet emotionally unavailable. I also apologized to my son and my church staff. I felt alive again.

Many of you reading this book have experienced loss on many levels. Let me ask you a few questions, "What does continuously rehearsing the loss, the "what ifs", and the effects of your loss solve?" I understand the right to personal disclosure of how you feel.

> Closure means bringing a **defined** ending point to an event in your life.

However, many times we are still stuck and that point of loss and need to progress in life. Life doesn't stop moving and neither should we. Bringing closure is about not staying in the moment. Bring closure to that divorce, hurt, layoff, failure, infidelity, criminal past, or whatever your loss may be. It is time for you to live.

I challenge you to make a decision. How do you want to proceed with life? Something inside of you wants more. It wants something different. God has something great in store for you, but you won't be able to experience it in its fullness trying to "play" it over old stuff. Start something new with a clean slate and watch what happens!!! To experience this kind of living, you have to bring closure to the period of your life that involved loss.

GETTING CLOSURE

So what does it actually mean to get closure? What if the person you need to reconcile with is dead? What if the person you need closure with doesn't think anything is wrong? What if they don't want any contact with you? How do you get closure in those situations? You may have unanswered questions and unresolved feelings. That is ok. You are not looking for feelings and answers to move forward. You are looking for direction from God. Again, closure doesn't mean you get an apology, an answer, or understanding. Closure means you bring a defined ending point to an event in your life. It means that you have ended that chapter of your life without taking the baggage of that situation with you. You leave the hurt, anger, frustration, and disappointment behind. You move on. You aren't ignoring the events that transpired, however, you are making a decision to move forward in spite of the loss. Some things may not make sense until later on. Focus on personal healing. Prepare for the life that lies ahead.

Shift

I love the story of Joshua. It is a perfect depiction of how God wants us to shift our lives after we have experienced a tough loss. Joshua 1:2 says, *"Moses my servant is dead. Now then, you and all these people, get ready to cross the Jordan River into the land I am about to give to them—to the Israelites." (NIV)* Basically, God said, "Listen, Moses is dead. Now I need you to get up and take this group of people and go to the land I promised you."

His statement did not downplay Moses' death. Rather, it shifted the focus from the death of Moses to the fulfillment of the promise made to Moses and the children of Israel. After loss and closure, you have to shift your focus. God didn't tell them not to grieve. God allows us to grieve, but He wants us to continue moving in the direction He is speaking.

I had the opportunity to move to the northeast for a year of my life. I lived in the great city of Philadelphia, PA. It was a great experience. I gained 50 pounds to prove it. On my first Sunday in the city, I attended a great church. The man who built it had passed away not long before my visit. My first Sunday was the first Sunday of the

Many people get stuck in what once was and miss out on the next phase of their life because they refuse to shift.

newly installed pastor. He had big shoes to fill! Was he to fill the founder's shoes or was he to carry the vision of the church further? The latter is correct. He was to carry the vision. There would never be another founder. The new pastor was phenomenal, but he had a tough time. Though he could never be the founding pastor, he was constantly being compared to him. One Sunday he got up and said the following in so many words, "Our founder is dead and I am your pastor now." That Sunday, he took his place as pastor. The people who wanted to go with him went with him and those who didn't were free to leave. That Sunday, I noticed a distinct shift in the church. At some point, we all must make this type of stand to experience a shift after loss. That marriage is *over*. That phase of your career is *over*. Your mistake is *over*. However, **your life is not over**. It is time for you to arise and cross the barrier separating you and your future. The promise of God *has not* changed. It is time to shift into your next place in life.

At some point, we all have to figure out when it is time to shift. Kenny Rogers had a song that included the following words, *"You've got to know when to hold 'em, know when to fold 'em, know when to walk away, know when to run"*. A part of life is knowing when to shut things down. It is not losing when you shut a thing down that has run its course. It is possible to ride a thing too long.

Everything runs its course. Many people get stuck in what once was and miss out on the next phase of their life because they refuse to shift. Life transitions are necessary. You have to learn when things have run their course and when it's time to move on. The transitional stages in our life our crucial. They are a critical stage in our life as winners. They are inevitable. We have to be willing to accept them and win at every stage of life.

Here are a few steps to help you realize and accept the shift in your life.

STEP 1: CHOOSE TO RECOVER

Make a decision to move on. Nothing happens in your life that you do not allow. God will not violate your free will. Choosing to recover is an act of your will. No one can do this for you. People can support you, but once you set your focus on shifting, the recovery process has begun. Choosing to recover doesn't mean you don't

> God **will not** violate your **free will**.

mourn, get sad, or have rough days. It simply means you are not going to stay in the place of loss. In Chapter 1, we discussed how to choose the thoughts we want to think. If we are not careful, our thoughts will cause us to believe we are crazy. We are responsible for choosing the thoughts that we think and developing a positive way of thinking. Our minds are a powerful tool from God. It can lead us to death or life. Sometimes the difference between a win and a loss is how we process information. Remember every thought has an end to it, so choose the ones you think wisely. Some thoughts may never leave you, you just don't have to follow them. After loss, thoughts of bitterness, offense, negativity, pessimism, and doubt may bombard us. We have to decide what we will think. If we think healing instead of pondering sickness, guess where we will eventually end up? Being healed. Many think they are unable to have strong faith because of constant worry, but here's the thing. Worry is just faith in the opposite direction. Worry is pondering a negative outcome. Faith is thinking and believing in a positive outcome.

STEP 2: GET A PROMISE FROM GOD AND STAND ON IT

Once you get a promise from God, relax and let God deliver the promise however He chooses. Many times our faith is hurt because people have not come through on their promises. Often, we may feel like God has let us down. Before he died, my brother and I would dream about him singing and his music going around the world. I remember God promising me that his music would be heard around the world. When he left this earth without me seeing evidence of God's promise, I was distraught. At his memorial service, a remarkable thing happened. As

> Worry is just faith in the **opposite direction**.

we sat and listened to three hours of people telling stories of my brother, one young man who recorded a song with my brother, got up and told the crowd of a village in Africa playing my brother's song. At that moment, God revealed that He had made good on His promise. We have to be open to how God performs his promises. What promises are you living by? If you don't have one, God will make you one, but you have to ask. Seek God for the answers you have about your life. Ask Him to reveal the promise and the purpose He has for you. Here's what I love about God. He is not a man that He should lie neither the Son of Man that He should repent. It may not look the way we think it should, but if God said it, He will see it through.

STEP 3: STRENGTHEN YOUR MIND

Each and every loss we endure impacts our confidence. Learn to separate your worth from your performance. We can make a mistake in life, but it doesn't make us an idiot, stupid, or an evil person. I learned this playing basketball in high school. My team had blown a twenty point lead. The other team had the ball and with seven seconds left in the game, I made a steal. The score was tied and I got to half court and panicked. I threw up a half-court shot. The ball hit the rim and I realized I had 3 seconds left. I am not sure how I did it, but I

> Learn to separate **your worth** from **your performance**.

got my own rebound and threw up another shot. I got fouled as I did this. My coach looked at me and told me to nail the shots. I had to forget the twenty point lead we blew, forget the bonehead shot that I threw up, and step to the line and win the game. Guess what? I nailed both free throws and we won the game. I made the city newspaper. I was a hero, for a day at least. The paper nor picture reflected my mistake. They only reflected the win. You have to keep this in mind as you approach life. When God restores things and makes them new, He only restores your wins. Developing the mind of Christ helps us to be mentally tough and recover from any loss.

STEP 4: DISTINGUISH BETWEEN FAITH AND FEELINGS

Feelings are where you are at the moment. Faith governs what direction you move in. Faith is believing in something greater than yourself and allowing God to empower you to heal and move forward. If you get your cues from your feelings, you will be all over the place. Your feelings will have you go from the mountain to the valley, honeymoon to divorce court, and debt free to bankruptcy with one thought. Faith is not a feeling. Faith is based on the Word of God which points you in a direction. Your faith directly impacts your confidence. I like to view faith as a muscle. The more you use it, the stronger it gets. Your feelings can deceive you, but faith will not. For instance, let's just say you have to forgive someone. You may find yourself angry at someone that you have forgiven. You may think you are having a setback. You have to remember forgiving someone is not a feeling. It is a move of faith that allows you to release the loss and move forward. Your emotions are triggered by memories. You have to remind your emotions of the decision that you have made to move forward in spite of how you feel. If you listen to your feelings, you will spend the rest of your life looking for the feeling of forgiveness.

STEP 5: MOVE FROM BLAME TO RESPONSIBILITY

If we always look to blame others, we will always lose. Honestly, when was the last time you heard someone say

> When we **blame others**, we hold them **responsible** for **our next win.**

my relationships is suffering because I am a jerk? I got fired because I have a horrible work ethic? Or, they switched my position because I oversold myself and couldn't do what was asked of me? Most of the time you hear the opposite. It is always somebody else's fault. You hear things like, if they weren't so stupid, I wouldn't be a jerk. I am being discriminated against. They don't like me because I am smarter than them. Everyone is jealous of me. When we place blame, we hold others responsible for our next win. You may never get an apology, answer, or acknowledgment, but those things don't have to stop you from healing and moving forward. People often say God did this (loss) to bring me closer to Him. Listen, if God takes your friends and family to bring you closer to Him, I am OUT!!! Many times when we suffer loss we think there has to be some hidden sin that God is judging. People say things like you reap what you sow, this is true, but always remember that God doesn't make anybody sin to get you back for the wrong you have done. We blame ourselves. We say, "I could have done more or I should have said more." We blame others. Crazy feelings and anger normally surface during loss. People turn on each other. Relationships are severed. Emotions are on high. The reason is everyone is looking for an answer. Although we are looking for answers, blame keeps us focused on the problem or the loss. There was an instance in the Bible where a man was born blind. The disciples asked Jesus who sinned that caused this man to be born blind. Jesus shifted the disciples from blame because they were searching for sin. He told them this happened so the work of God can be displayed through Him. What message does this story hold for believers today? That the most important thing in any situation, is the solution. When you shift from blame to responsibility, you begin looking for solutions.

SHIFT GEARS

You are resilient! You possess the ability to shift in every season of your life. Your resilient nature is like a thermostat to every situation in your life versus a thermometer. Thermometers give you the reading of the current condition. It is always accurate. It says what it sees. However, you are not guided by the current reading.

You are a thermostat. Thermostats don't say what they see, they see what they say. You have the ability to shift any environment. You can set a thermostat to whatever temperature you desire for it to be. Your faith does the same thing. It applies what you believe to a situation. Your situation may currently read broke, sick, depressed, or without hope. However, you can set it to prosperity, healing, and joy. When you set your faith in a direction, all of Heaven begins to shift your environment on your behalf.

After bringing closure to a loss, you need to shift! It is time to put your life in another gear! You may have to gear down to regroup or you may need to take things up a notch. The whole point of shifting is that you don't stop; you adjust. At worst, go into neutral and allow the people around you to love on you and support you until you can get back up to speed. Whatever you do, don't park. Parked cars don't move, neither do parked spirits or mentalities.

reFrame Your Life

I n most settings, I use my iPad to teach. One particular Sunday, my battery was running low. I began to panic. It was running low during the first service. I still had to preach the second service. I didn't have enough time between services to give it the full charge it needed. In the middle of my panic, I had an idea. I decided to send my sermon to someone who had an iPad. My iPad eventually lost power, but I was still able to finish my sermon. I simply used someone else's iPad. In my panic, I had to realize that my sermon was not in the iPad, my iPad was merely the vehicle I used to see my sermon. My iPad may have died, but my sermon didn't. When dealing with loss, we must take this same approach to life. Our purpose is still alive after loss. We simply need a new plan or a new place. Unfortunately, many shut down after failed attempts of trying something. The good news is; we can still try again after loss. We simply need to reframe our lives.

Have you ever had to reframe a picture? In reframing, you realize that there is absolutely nothing wrong with the picture, it just needs a new frame. The prefix re- means "to do again". After loss, we simply need to find our place in life again.

It is important to know that you still have value, and there is still potential in your

> Your purpose **is still alive** after loss.

life even after a tough loss. Your experience does not change the integrity of what you lost. Marriage, ministry, love, friendship, business, health or whatever you lost is still a possibility. Your marriage may have been bad, but marriage is still God's idea. There's no such thing as marriage problems. The real issue is people with problems get married and bring those problems into the marriage. Business and prosperity are still God's idea. You don't have to take an oath of poverty and disavow your desire to drive economic change because you failed in business or financially. You

> **Admit** that you **are not** the person you were before loss. **Refuse** to **retreat** to how things **used to be**.

have to simply reframe your life. A big question most people have after loss is, "What's next?" Having closure and shifting your mindset ignites your passion again. To find your place in life again, you must reframe. You have to admit that you are not the person you were before loss, so you can't go back to things the way they used to be. You have to figure out where you fit. Here are six principles to think about as you reframe your life and live in your resilience.

PRINCIPLE 1: RECONNECT

The one thing that isn't altered by loss is your purpose. Your purpose is what you were created to be and do before you ever experienced a thing. Purpose was there before you ever got hurt, made a mistake, or lost a loved one. Loss exposes what is important to you. Your values are different after you experience loss. You begin to notice that you were focusing on things that didn't matter. Loss has a crazy way of eliminating the fluff in our lives. You have to view loss in light of your purpose. Reframe your life by reconnecting to your purpose. Don't view your life in light of your experiences. View your life in light of your purpose and the promises God has spoken over your life. Begin to focus your time on areas that will make a significant impact in your life.

PRINCIPLE 2: REFOCUS

To refocus, you have to put life into a new perspective. Loss may impact your ministry, daily life, your line of work, and how you see things, but it doesn't change your purpose. Perhaps you have been abused, and you have decided to spend your life helping other victims of abuse. This is tremendous. However, understand that your purpose is not to help abuse victims. That is a ministry you have taken on. Your purpose may be to help people in general. You just chose to direct that purpose in an area you are passionate about, but you must not lose focus on why you were created. There are others areas of life that are worthy of attention as well. Can I be honest? A

> Loss has a **crazy way** of **eliminating the fluff** in our lives.

lot of us who experience loss become focused on the loss ONLY. If we are not careful, that passion that is meant to help us can put us at odds with others who are pursuing other worthwhile endeavors. We end up having a narrow view of life. God exposes things to us that are not being addressed; not as an indictment on anyone else, but to create a space for us to do what we are called to do. It is very easy to run off the momentum of emotion. You can take on a "save the world mentality" and burn out easily. If your momentum is pain, what will drive you once you are healed? Your purpose should be the fuel that drives you through any situation. The great thing about God is that He allows us to use our purpose to help those who have experienced loss.

PRINCIPLE 3: reTHINK

As a result of experience, I have begun to rethink my approach on certain things in life. The best time to rethink life is immediately after a loss. Ask yourself. Are the current systems in your life producing what is in your heart? Are you in survival mode because of your experiences? Understand that is not the way to live. Resilient people are more than survivors; we are overcomers. You don't have to live that way. Find out what you want out of life and set your course in that direction.

PRINCIPLE 4: reNEW

There is a church website that I frequently visit to watch their pastor's sermons. I got a message one day that my browser was out of date. Since my browser was out of date, I was not getting the full advantage of their new website. Their website had changed but my

view hadn't. This is the way

> **Don't have an outdated
> view of a new reality.**

we tend to view life after

loss. We have an outdated

view of a new reality. This is why you need to renew after loss. To

renew something means you refresh it. You could be out of touch

with the industry you are in. If you have taken a hiatus from a

particular field because of loss, it is important to renew your

thinking to the current trends. You are still smart and have the

aptitude to win, but you need to enlighten yourself on how to

currently win. Things change quickly. Each day people are creating

more efficient ways to do things. Could your approach be a little

outdated? Even in your personal life you need to refresh. Make sure

you are reading, resting, and relaxing to keep yourself fresh.

PRINCIPLE 5: reFORM

A reform is in order after loss. Some loss is self-inflicted. In cases

of self-inflicted loss, you need a heart change. Your value system, character, and integrity need to be reformed. I love the story of David. The Bible says God declared David as a man after His own heart. However, David was also a

> Your **behavior** is a byproduct of what you **believe**.

man that made mistakes. After a great mistake, David prayed an incredible prayer. He asked God to create in him a clean heart and renew a right spirit in him. David said he wanted truth in the inward parts. This should be the prayer of anyone seeking reformation. Our mistakes do not define us. We often try to fix our mistakes by changing our behavior. Your behavior is a byproduct of what you believe. You believe with your heart. When God changes your heart, your belief system changes and your behavior naturally corrects itself.

PRINCIPLE 6: REVIEW

My prayer is that over the course of reading this book, something has connected with you. Perhaps you are developing your comeback plan for life, or maybe you are just dreaming of what your life can look like. I want to encourage you to write out your plan and submit it to the Lord. Develop a vision for your life and review it often. You may have experienced some difficult losses in life, but you don't have to remain there. For the living, there is hope. As long as you have life left in your body, you have the opportunity to get right everything you got wrong. Things may look bleak. It may seem like there is no hope. I want to challenge you to look again. Several stories in the Bible show how the Lord challenged His people to look again. There was the story of the blind man who opened his eyes and saw men as trees. So the Lord prayed for him again. When he *"looked again"* he saw men as they were. Then, there was Elisha's servant who first thought the enemy had them surrounded until he was prayed for and when he *"looked again"* he saw angels surrounding his enemies and was reminded that they that be with us are more than they that be with them. *Look again!!* Whether or not we realize it, one of satan's tactics is to twist the truth and get you to believe a lie based on how things look. I want to challenge you today to *"look again"*. There is more to life than what you see. Don't give up because things don't look right, look again. Don't allow someone else's issues to shape your view of life, *look again*. If God ever made you a promise, your reality must line up with HIS Word, *look again*. Look through the eyes of faith today. All God has is not all you see. *Look again.* I want to leave you with the following scriptures and thoughts. 2 Timothy 2:13 says, *"If we are faithless [do not believe and are untrue to Him], He remains true (faithful to His Word and His righteous character), for He cannot deny Himself."* Even in your doubting moments and your moments of unfaithfulness; God is not unfaithful to His Word over your life. God will not deny Himself the opportunity to perform His Word in your life. You have grace in your situation. Repent and get back in faith to receive the promise of God. **You are resilient.**

References

Paul, R. (2002). Viewing the body and grief complications: the role of visual confirmation in grief reconciliation. *Complicated grieving and bereavement: understanding and treating people experiencing loss. Amityville, New York: Baywood.*

James, J. W., & Friedman, R. (2009). *The grief recovery handbook.* Harper Collins.

Made in the USA
Middletown, DE
17 March 2022

62798066R00071